21st Century Junior Library

DISCOVER THE DIRE WOLF

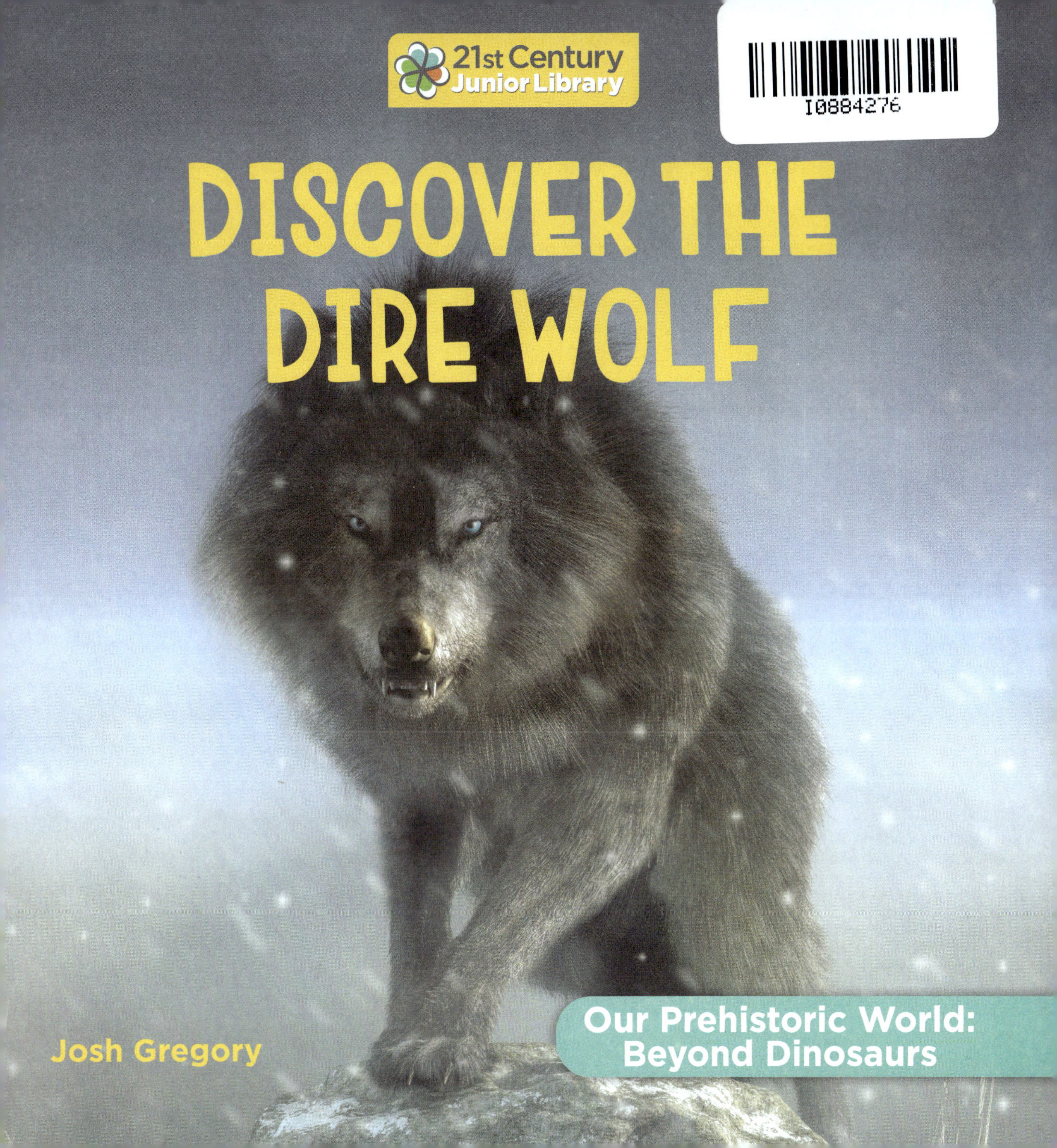

Our Prehistoric World: Beyond Dinosaurs

Josh Gregory

Published in the United States of America by:

CHERRY LAKE PRESS
2395 South Huron Parkway, Suite 200, Ann Arbor, Michigan 48104
www.cherrylakepress.com

Reading Adviser: Beth Walker Gambro, MS, Ed., Reading Consultant, Yorkville, IL

Photo and Illustration Credits: © Daniel Eskridge/Shutterstock, cover, title page; © ROMAN UCHYTEL/SCIENCE PHOTO LIBRARY, 5; © serchio25/Deviant Art, 6; © MAURICIO ANTON/SCIENCE PHOTO LIBRARY, 7; NPS illustration by Benji Paysnoe/Wikimedia Commons via Public Domain, 8-9; © ROMAN UCHYTEL/SCIENCE PHOTO LIBRARY, 10; © Nataba/iStock.com, 11; © Aunt Spray/Shutterstock, 12; © Catmando/Shutterstock, 14-15; © Shahfahd/Shutterstock, 16; James St. John, CC BY 2.0 via Wikimedia Commons, 17; James St. John, CC BY 2.0 via Wikimedia Commons, 18; © Courtesy of Colossal Biosciences, 20-21

Cherry Lake Press is an imprint of Cherry Lake Publishing Group.

Library of Congress Cataloging-in-Publication Data has been filed and is available at catalog.loc.gov.

Cherry Lake Press would like to acknowledge the work of the Partnership for 21st Century Learning, a Network of Battelle for Kids. Please visit Battelle for Kids online for more information.

Printed in the United States of America

CHERRY LAKE PRESS

CONTENTS

WHAT WAS A DIRE WOLF?

You've probably seen all kinds of dogs and wolves. But you haven't seen all of them. Long ago, a **species** called the dire wolf roamed Earth. It lived between 250,000 to 10,000 years ago. The name *dire wolf* comes from Latin words meaning "terrible wolf." But this doesn't mean the wolves were bad. It means they were huge and scary!

Dire wolves lived during the Late Pleistocene epoch. Their prey included animals like the Columbian mammoth.

Dire wolves had a lot in common with gray wolves. But they actually weren't close relatives. Some scientists don't think dire wolves were wolves at all. They think dire wolves were their own kind of **canid**. For thousands of years, dire wolves lived alongside gray wolves. Both were common in what is now North and South America.

Gray wolves (left) looked similar to dire wolves (right). But dire wolves were usually a bit bigger and stronger.

Create!

What do you think your hometown looked like in the time of dire wolves? Draw a picture. Include as many details as you can.

Dire wolves died out around 10,000 years ago. Scientists think it was because the large animals the wolves hunted started to disappear. Dire wolves were not good at hunting smaller, faster prey. Gray wolves were better at hunting smaller prey. That may be why they survived and dire wolves didn't.

WHAT DID A DIRE WOLF LOOK LIKE?

Dire wolves looked a lot like the wolves and wild dogs that live today. They walked on four legs. They had mouths filled with sharp teeth. Fur covered their bodies. Scientists think their fur was probably gray or brown.

Dire wolves probably had gray or brown fur to blend in with their surroundings. It likely helped them surprise prey.

Dire wolves were bigger than today's wolves. They weighed about 130 to 150 pounds (59 to 68 kilograms). That's about 1.25 times the size of a gray wolf. A dire wolf's body was also shaped a little differently. It had shorter legs than today's wolves. It also had a bigger head. This gave it a powerful bite.

Dire wolves used their more powerful bite to take down larger prey.

Look!

Do you have a pet dog? Are there dogs in your neighborhood? Give them a look. How are they like wolves? How are they different?

Evidence shows that dire wolves likely chose a mate and stayed with that one mate for life.

HOW DID A DIRE WOLF LIVE?

Dire wolves probably lived together in large family groups called **packs**. This is also how wolves and wild dogs live today. Pack members protect each other. They help each other raise pups. Group living helps keep them safe from **predators**.

Packs of wolves also work together to hunt **prey**. This practice allows them to hunt bigger animals. Dire wolves probably hunted wild horses. They probably also ate large animals like ground sloths, camels, and bison. They used their powerful jaws to attack. Sometimes they might not have been able to find enough live prey. Then they might have **scavenged** for dead animals to eat.

Ask Questions!

How is hunting large prey different than hunting small prey? What skills would dire wolves have needed? How can you find answers to these questions? Who can help you?

Sharp teeth and claws helped dire wolves take down and eat large animals.

The first dire wolf bones were found in 1854 in Indiana. They were next found in Nebraska.

How do we know so much about animals that lived so long ago? By studying **fossils**! Thousands of dire wolf skeletons have been found at the La Brea Tar Pits in California. Dire wolf fossils have also been found from Alaska all the way to South America.

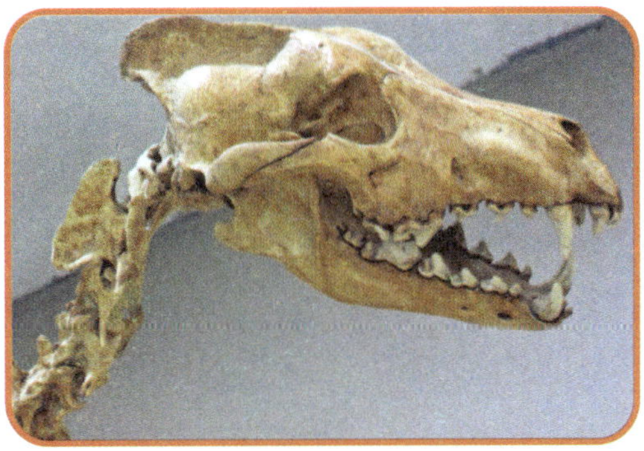

Dire wolf fossils have been found in North and South America.

These fossils tell us where dire wolves lived. They also give clues about what they ate and how they lived. There is still a lot to learn, though. Scientists will keep studying dire wolf fossils for a long time.

Make a Guess!

Dire wolves hunted prehistoric horses. These horses once lived in North America. When Europeans arrived in the 1500s, there were no more horses. They brought horses over from Europe. What do you think happened to the horses that were once there?

In 2025, a group of scientists claimed they had brought back dire wolves. They changed the **genes** of gray wolf pups to do this. This change made the pups bigger than normal. The new pups might look a little like dire wolves did. But most scientists agree that they are not really dire wolves. A species can't come back after it is **extinct**.

Think!

Scientists used ancient dire wolf DNA to bring three wolf pups into the world in 2024 and 2025. These pups are not 100 percent dire wolf, but they have a lot of dire wolf traits! Is it a good idea to bring back extinct animals? What could happen? What animals would you want to see come back?

This image shows Romulus and Remus. They are two of the pups born from the dire wolf DNA experiment.

GLOSSARY

canid (KAA-nuhd) scientific group of animals that includes wolves, jackals, coyotes, foxes, and dogs

extinct (ik-STINKT) no longer found living anywhere on Earth

fossils (FAH-suhlz) remains or traces of plants, animals, and other living things that have been preserved as rocks

genes (JEENZ) material in cells that is passed down by parents; genes determine how offspring will look and grow

packs (PAKS) groups of animals living as a unit

predators (PREH-duh-tuhrz) animals that hunt other animals for food

prey (PRAY) animals that are hunted by other animals for food

scavenged (SKA-venjd) searched for dead animals as a food source

species (SPEE-sheez) group of living things that share many characteristics and can mate and produce offspring

FIND OUT MORE

Books

Neuenfeldt, Elizabeth. *Dire Wolves.* Minneapolis, MN: Bellwether Media, 2025.

Somervill, Barbara A. *Gray Wolf.* Ann Arbor, MI: Cherry Lake Publishing, 2008.

Websites

With an adult, learn more online with these suggested searches.

National Park Service: Dire Wolf

Learn more about the places where dire wolf fossils have been found.

San Diego Natural History Museum: Dire Wolf

Find out more about the reasons dire wolves went extinct.

INDEX

ABOUT THE AUTHOR

Josh Gregory is the author of more than 250 books for young readers, covering everything from video games and technology to dinosaurs and U.S. history. He lives in Chicago, Illinois.

About Paleoartists

Paleoartists bring the prehistoric world to life! They work with scientists, paleontologists, museums, and their own research to recreate living things from long, long ago. **Mark Witton** is one paleoartist featured in this series. He has been studying prehistoric creatures for over 20 years! **Brian Engh** is another. He builds sculptures, too. He designs and builds whole exhibits. He started Living Relic Productions.